God is Enough

by M.E. Louis

•••

Distributed by Bublish, Inc.
bublish.com

•••

Cover design by AM Design Studios

ISBN-10: 1-946229-77-6

ISBN-13: 978-1-946229-77-9

Table of Contents

Acknowledgments .... *v*

Introduction *1*

Chapter One
Deep Grief *3*

Chapter Two
Loneliness *17*

Chapter Three
Healing *25*

Chapter Four
God Stories *39*

Chapter Five
Thriving *47*

Chapter Six
Change and Purpose *61*

Chapter Seven
Providing Comfort Do's and Don'ts............................*69*

About the Author *73*

Closing Thoughts..*75*

List of Books to Help Cope with Grief......................*79*

Bible Verses to Guide You *87*

ACKNOWLEDGMENTS

---◇---

First and foremost, I want to thank my Savior, Jesus Christ, who has been my guide since I was sixteen years old. He brought my husband, Bob into my life during college, and we shared our lives together for 33 amazing years. As much as my heart aches and as deafening as the silence is in our house, I am so thankful for the wonderful, precious memories I was able to create with the love of my life.

Secondly, it has been said that it takes a village to raise a child. In my estimation, it takes at least that to walk beside a devastated widow and teach her how to rejoin life without her lifelong partner.

The members of this village will NEVER know the important role they played in my life.

These members consisted of a biblical counselor, massage therapist, family, friends, co-workers and boss, church staff and members, neighbors, and fellow widows.

There are three people that I would like to thank by name. They are TJ, who was the first person to arrive at my house that dreadful day that I lost Bob. She disposed of the ladder and rope that my husband used to take his life, and remained by my side throughout the obligatory police investigation. She also acted as my chauffeur to any destination I needed to reach. My Mom, widowed two years prior to my husband's death, provided comfort by her presence—either staying at my house or letting me crash at hers. My now best friend, Mom's numerous phone calls and willingness to travel with me have been a precious gift. Peggy—who traveled out of state to stay with me for my first week alone—called frequently and sent presents on "hard" days like Valentine's Day, Christmas, my birthday and Bob's and our anniversary. To this day, we continue to plan things to do together each August 7—the day I lost my husband and best friend.

Thank you all for making such a profound difference in my life!

To my readers, thank you for making time to take this journey with me. It is certainly a journey that no one wants to take. May the pages of this book encourage you, resonate with you, challenge you and most of all introduce you to the ONE who walks this journey with you like no one else can. His name is Jesus.

INTRODUCTION

In the midst of the most horrific event of my life, God showed me that HE IS ENOUGH. He met me where I was. **"The LORD is near to the broken-hearted and saves the crushed in spirit." (Psalm 34:18 ESV)** He loved me cnough to not let me stay brokenhearted. **"He lifted me out of the slimy pit, out of the mud and mire; He set my feet on a rock and gave me a firm place to stand." (Psalm 40:2 NIV)**

I am not the same person today that I was prior to my husband's suicide. Now, I know God in a way that I have never known Him before. After my husband's death, God did a complete makeover of my life. He required me to take several important steps, and showed me how to:

1. Focus on God's promises in the midst of my very difficult circumstance.
2. Dwell on God's character in spite of my pain.
3. Realize that there is purpose in my suffering.

God's work in making me over was a two-year process. What I learned during that challenging period is now an integral part of my lifestyle. God's activity in my daily life is visible; I need only to look for it. These words are now incorporated into my life: **"In the morning, LORD, you hear my voice; in the morning I lay my requests before you and wait expectantly." (Psalm 5:3 NIV)**

For me, the third step was the most difficult to accept. However, over the past two years, I have come to the same conclusion that Yvonne Bibby, my close friend and veteran missionary, did when she wrote in her book, *WAKE UP! RETURN TO GOD,* (2015), "There will be times of suffering in the world when pain and sorrow fill our days. As we come to God in our suffering, He reveals a part of Himself we have never known before. As we patiently endure, seeking God instead of His answers, He will come to us and renew our hearts toward Him."

CHAPTER ONE

DEEP GRIEF

"Blessed be the God, and Father of our Lord Jesus Christ, the Father of mercies and God of all comfort; who comforts us in all our affliction so we may be able to comfort those who are in any affliction with the comfort with which we ourselves are comforted by God."

2 Corinthians 1:3, 4 (NASB)

On August 5, 2013 my husband started a new job. I packed his lunch to take with him that first day. Bob liked when I would write a note and include it in his lunch bag. This is the note I wrote that day.

Dear Tate,

I hope your first day is a good one. I look forward to hearing all about it tonight! I am so proud of you. Your determination and persistence helped make today a reality. I love you very, very much. See you tonight, Boo

Two days later, August 7, 2013, was the day my life changed forever. The phone rang early this Wednesday morning. It was my husband's boss, Neil, asking if my husband was home. I thought to myself, *What a strange question?*

Several hours earlier, while it was still dark and I was in bed, my husband had kissed me goodbye. "He should be with you," I told Neil.

"I know," he responded. "That is why I am calling. He always gets here a half hour early, and he is not here. Is he there?"

> August 7, 2013 was the day my life changed forever.

I put my bathrobe on with the cordless phone in hand and walked downstairs in search of my husband. He was not in the house. I looked out the back door and spotted his car parked in the driveway. Upon seeing my husband's car, I remember responding to Neil, "That is not good."

"Is there somewhere special he would go?" Neil asked.

"No."

"Why don't you walk outside and look from one end of the yard to the other."

Okay, I thought to myself.

I started scanning the backyard, turning my head to the left-side of the yard lined with crepe myrtles in full bloom, then the center, and finally to the right-side of the yard. When I saw my husband, he was wearing his pajamas. He had been standing on a small step stool and was now on his knees so it first appeared as if he was sitting on the stool. Then, suddenly in disbelief I saw the yellow rope around his neck and realized I was seeing my husband of 33 years hanging from a tree. I screamed his name as I collapsed on the picnic table like a limp rag doll.

> I collapsed on the picnic tables.

"Neil, he hung himself!"

Neil asked if I wanted to call 911 or should he.

"I want you to call them, Neil." He then placed me on hold.

The next words I heard were, "They want you to cut him down."

"Why?"

"There might be a chance that he is still alive," Neil urged.

Like a robot, I told Neil I was going to put the phone down to go inside and get some scissors. Even though I knew my husband was dead—his tongue was blue and sticking out of his mouth and his face was as white as a ghost—I did what Neil told me to do. I was shaking and everything seemed to be so quiet and still. It was like I was living in a dream and everything was happening in slow motion. It seemed that my mind was taking hours to process what was happening.

When I replay this horrific scene in my head, I realize that I was completely incapable of processing what I was seeing. Even as I cut my husband down from the tree, I braced myself against his body, so he didn't fall face down and break his glasses. My plan did not work, and he fell down on his face. It took all the strength I had to turn him over on his back.

I returned to the picnic table, sat down and picked up the phone to thank Neil for his help. At that point, I heard the sirens. It is an unnerving feeling to hear sirens, and know they are coming to your house!

There is a fire station two blocks from our house so a fire truck was the first vehicle to arrive. Next an ambulance, followed by 3 police cars. I stayed in the backyard long enough to ask the emergency responders if Bob was dead and they confirmed what I already knew. I walked back to the picnic table in a state of shock and thought, "Who should I call?" There were three people I decided to call. I first called Mom. She lives an hour away so I knew it would be awhile before she arrived. Next, I called TJ who lives just minutes from my house. She asked if I was by myself and I said I was. She responded, "I will be right there." The third person I called was my boss. I don't remember what I said to any of these people.

Next, came two separate police agencies asking me lots of questions for hours. They were very polite and respectful but I remember shaking as I was answering their questions. TJ sat on the couch beside me for the entire interrogation. I was thankful that she was there. I couldn't imagine going through that by myself!

Over and over—with all its absurdities—I have replayed this scene in my head.

"Why did this happen?" I recall saying, "God, You could have stopped this! Why didn't You?"

I was tormented and wrestled with unanswered questions like this for several weeks. How could I reconcile my husband's suicide with the fact that God's Son, Jesus, loved my husband enough to die for him? My husband had accepted Jesus as his Savior, and had lived his life desiring to serve Him. My husband closed his eyes on earth and opened them in Heaven!

"God loved the world so much that He gave His only Son, that everyone who has faith in Him may not die, but have eternal life. For God did not send His Son into the world to be its Judge, but to be its Savior." (John 3:16, 17 GNT)

I concluded that a loving God chose not to stop the suicide. I don't know why. What I do know is that God knows everything, including the day each of us will die.

"A person's days are determined; You have decreed the number of his months and have set limits he cannot exceed." (Job 14:5 NIV)

"You saw me before I was born. The days allotted to me had all been recorded in Your book before any of them ever began." (Psalm 139:16 GNT)

Shortly after Bob's death, God used Psalm 139:16 powerfully in my life. This verse had the power to remove all the guilt I carried about what I should or shouldn't have done to prevent Bob from taking his life. This verse gave me much needed comfort and peace to know there was nothing I could do. Psalm 139:16 was pivotal to my healing and was a huge step toward my acceptance of God's will for my life moving forward. I was shocked by my husband's death, but God was not. God already knew that my husband would choose to end his life on that Wednesday morning in the summer of 2013. God had even orchestrated the call from my husband's boss Neil. Did I mention Neil had only known Bob for three days?

Everything that I had known changed the day Bob took his life, and it would NEVER be the same again. Day after day life bombarded into my painful existence.

How dare life continue when for me, it had come to an abrupt halt!

It felt as if I were standing in the middle of a merry-go-round with life circling continuously around me. I was wandering in a fog with no direction. NOTHING had prepared me for THIS.

Every time I closed my eyes, I saw my husband hanging from that tree in our backyard. I could not sleep. I had flashbacks for months. I sought out a biblical counselor because I knew I needed to process what had happened in order to begin healing. I wanted counsel from someone who was professionally trained, but also offered guidance from the Bible.

"Lord, to whom shall we go? You have the words of eternal life."(John 6:68 NIV)

"I am the LORD, and there is no other; Besides Me there is no God." (Isaiah 45:5 NASB)

"For such is God, our God forever and ever; He will guide us until death." (Psalm 48:14 NASB).

I wanted help from the only One who could give it.

The counselor offered assistance with the flashbacks. She asked me to think about a picture of my husband that I had in our house—one in which he looked very happy. I got that image in my mind. It was a picture of Bob and I dressed in our UNC gear, with me

9

wearing a BEAT DUKE button, taken inside the Dean E. Smith Center. This photo was shot minutes after UNC defeated Duke to win the 2010 -11 conference regular season championship. Bob and I are each holding up the number one finger to symbolize UNC's first place in the ACC. To this day, whenever I look at that picture, I can feel clearly in my mind what Bob's jacket feels like and how his arm around my waist feels. The biblical counselor then instructed me that every time I had a flashback I was to immediately focus my mind on that picture. "Even as happy as he appears in that picture," she emphatically stated, "he is now happier than he has ever been because he is in Heaven."

Wow... amazing.... so simple.... yet so profound! Her suggestion worked, and the flashbacks eventually subsided.

Additionally, the counselor asked me to focus each day on only three things:

1. God's character
2. God's promises
3. The reality that there is purpose in my suffering

"Each day is an opportunity for you to rely on God's character and/or His promises," the counselor told me. "Record daily how you did this."

Since there was no plumb line for my experience, I chose to do whatever the counselor asked me to do. For many weeks, I would quote God's promises aloud, just to gain the strength to get out of bed. I recall using these two verses over and over to help me through the mornings.

"I can do all things through Him who strengthens me." (Philippians 4:13 NASB)

"I love you, LORD, my strength." (Psalms 18:1 NIV)

After recording daily my work on the three focus points for six months, I discovered my life verse.

"In the morning, LORD, you hear my voice; in the morning I lay my requests before you and wait expectantly." (Psalm 5:3 NIV)

What I mean by the term "life verse" is that it directed my focus and outlook each and every day. It stated in black and white what I had been doing the past six months as well as what I continue to do to work through my grief. What I found in this Bible verse was relief—the pressure was taken off of me. Without my husband, I had grown weary of making all the decisions on my own day after day. Psalm 5:3 directs me to give all of my concerns directly to God. What a huge relief this concept was for a weary widow.

There is a lot packed into Psalm 5:3. First, the verse tells to whom to go…the LORD. Then, the verse explains that He hears what I say. The Bible verse instructs me to tell God my requests and wait expectantly to see how He will act. The word "expectantly" implies that I must look forward and wait for God to make something happen.

This Bible verse radically changed me as a person. In the midst of intense, heart-wrenching pain, I began to look for God's activity in my life. The verse gave me "one thing" to focus upon, and at that point in my life that was about all I had the energy to do. For two years, I recorded how God acted in my life. The results were mind boggling!

How did I determine it was God's activity? His divine activity was unique, personal, unexpected and often met a need or request that I had placed in His hands. As Bob would often say, "You can't make this up!" What he meant by that statement was that what took place could only be explained as the work of God. Psalm 5:3 gives specific instructions about how to live your life...one day at a time....one step at a time. Each day, you must look expectantly for His actions in your life.

Speaking of one step at a time, it took me at least two-and-a-half years to re-engage fully into life. The first two years, I was in survival mode, nothing more. Five years after my husband's suicide, I am finally thriving! The first year after his death, I was just going through the motions. I did what I needed to do to stay alive; that was all. I was in a state of severe shock. I was an automaton with no emotions beyond intense grief. I had a box of tissues in every room of my house as well as in my purse and car. Those days are a blur now. I vividly remember going three entire days in a row without crying. It was such a huge feat! There are so many things I can't recall from the first year. Most of the things I do recall are very painful—like daily conversations. I dreaded each and every time that a friend or acquaintance asked, "How are you?" I certainly was not going to say, "Fine," when I was so completely and utterly sad. I decided to answer honestly, but quickly realized that many people didn't slow down long enough to actually hear my response. It was also obvious that many people experienced extreme discomfort with someone else's grief.

I also remember, loving, rainy days because then I would not be inundated with comments like, "Isn't it a lovely day?" Clearly, at that point in my life none of the days were lovely! I avoided eating in restaurants because I did not want to hear laughter or see families eating together. I avoided the neighborhood grocery store because I often shopped there with my husband. I had a difficult time going to sleep in an empty bed. I missed talking with my best friend and spending time with him. The laughter that often filled our house had been replaced by a deafening silence.

In addition to all the emotional changes in my life, I also had to learn many new skills. I had crash courses in bill paying, developing a budget, putting a new roof on the house, adding a garage, replacing rotten Masonite boards with Hardie Plank and the list goes on and on. This was my new normal, and I did not like it or want it. I recall some friends taking me to breakfast and asking what they could do to support me. "You can bring my husband back," I responded. For 33 years, I had been one half of a couple. Then, suddenly, I was single. I could go on for pages detailing the changes that accompanied the loss of my husband. Suffice it to say, EVERYTHING was an enormous adjustment.

The best way to describe my mental state at that time was deep despair. The sense of loss was a bottomless cavern. Becca, a paralegal, was my driver for weeks as we made multiple visits to the courthouse. She knew things I knew nothing about which was a huge help to me. She even arranged for someone from Social Security to call me at home to discuss possible benefits.

Bob was 6'2" and weighed 178 pounds. When he was cremated, his ashes weighed 10 pounds. Needless to say all of his ashes would not fit in the urns I saw at the funeral home. I ended up putting his ashes in a large UNC cookie jar container. The first morning Becca came to the door I was carrying the cookie jar because I wanted to take Bob with us in her van (I knew his spirit was in heaven, I just felt like he was with me). The following morning Becca asked, "Is Bob going with us this morning?" To which I replied, "No, he is staying home today. I am mad at him!"

I recall one day Becca driving me to the Division of Motor Vehicles to transfer the title of the car from

Bob's name to mine. What Becca did not know was that the week before Bob drove us to the same DMV office to show me how to get tags for the car. That was something he always took care of and at the time he explained that he might not always be around, so it would be good for me to know how to do this. Needless to say when I walked into the DMV office with Becca and into the same room where Bob and I had been only a few days earlier I lost it. I cried uncontrollably. Becca and I walked down to the basement in search of a Mountain Dew. I was drinking a lot of Mountain Dews as my coping mechanism. Once I found one, I sat down and tried to regain my composure. When I did, we returned to the counter to complete the form necessary for a title transfer. I needed to write my name and his name in four places on the form. Even this simple task was daunting to me and I was unsuccessful in completing the form correctly. I was given a new form to complete and requested that the DMV employee show me one at a time where I needed to write each piece of information. I would write what she said and then hand it back to her so she could show me where to sign, and I repeated this request four times in order to complete this simple task.

Grief also interrupted my eating. At first, I could only eat cold items. For weeks, I subsisted on banana and cheese sandwiches, yogurt, fresh fruit, milk and Mountain Dew. A dear friend offered to buy my favorite ice cream from a local store that was famous for its homemade ice cream. I agreed, since it was a cold item. I attempted to eat it to no avail. I found this to be very strange! Bob and I frequented this same ice cream store and we both had our favorite flavors. Mine was Dark Almond and Bob's was Brownie Batter. We went so often that we would argue in the car about who would go in, saying to each other, " I went in last time!"

CHAPTER TWO

LONELINESS

"You are with me."

Psalm 23:4 (NKJV)

I did a lot of journaling after Bob's death. I would describe my feelings, struggles, and range of emotions as I traveled into unknown territory. This daily ritual helped me process the nightmare I was living. I would start each day by reading a passage in the Bible and then journal about what I read.

Two months after my husband's suicide I was reading Matthew 26:36-40 which states, **"Then Jesus came with them to a place called Gethsemane, and said to His disciples, 'Sit here while I go over there and pray.' And He took with Him Peter and the two sons of Zebedee, and began to be grieved and distressed. Then He said to them, 'My soul is deeply grieved to the point of death; remain here and keep watch with**

Me.' And He went a little beyond them, and fell on His face and prayed… And He came to the disciples and found them sleeping, and said to Peter, 'So you men could not keep watch with me for one hour?'"

I can definitely relate to Jesus's statement of being "crushed with grief to the point of death." I know what it feels like to wonder if I'll ever get out from underneath it. I see that Jesus also understands the loneliness of grief that has at times overwhelmed me. He asked his friends to stay awake and alert. Even those closest to Him could not stay awake in some of the most agonizing hours of his life. People often say to me, "Is there anything I can do for you?" "No". Not only is there nothing they can do, there is no way they can comprehend the enormous wound in my heart and how lonely I feel. I know what it feels like for my soul to be crushed with grief to the point that I wonder if I can survive it. I feel forsaken and abandoned by those I hoped would be there in this difficult time.

I am thankful for these Bible verses in Matthew that show me Jesus understands. They offer comfort for this lonely, heart-broken widow.

The healing part of journaling is that it gave me an outlet to express my feelings to God like I was writing a letter to Him. My writing was full of honest and raw emotion that was released as I wrote.

"During the days of Jesus' life on earth, He offered up prayers and petitions with fervent cries and tears to the one who could save Him from death, and He

was heard because of His reverent submission. Son though He was, He learned obedience from what He suffered." (Hebrews 5:7,8 NIV)

After reading these passages in the Bible I wrote:

One of the hardest parts of trusting God has been reconciling the fact that God had the power to stop Bob from committing suicide, but He chose not to do so. Hebrews 5:7–8 has helped me as I wrestle with this. In these verses I see the fully human, fully God facing the cross and crying out to the Father, who has the power to make another way, but chooses not to do so. I see Jesus submit to God's plan, a plan that included suffering and death. Jesus wrestled with God's plan to redeem the world through His death on the cross. It helps because I, too, have struggled with God's plan for my life.

Father, I believe by faith that Your plans for my life are perfect, although this has caused me so much pain! May I continue to follow You.

The word loneliness encompasses more than being alone. It is attached to an emotion, like feeling sad or depressed. I wasn't lonely because I was alone; I was lonely because I missed my husband. I missed talking over our days, discussing vacation plans, walking our dog in the neighborhood, eating together, and on and on and on. I missed the intimacy of our relationship. For the first time in my life, I fully understood how someone could be in a crowd of people and still feel lonely.

For months, I would go daily to a local department store after work because I did not want to go home. Why? It wasn't because I was afraid to be alone in my home. I just couldn't face the reality that my husband would no longer be there with me. For the first two weeks following my husband's death, people would spend the night at my house to keep me company. It was nice to have someone in the house with me—someone with whom I could converse.

After two weeks, I decided I would try to stay all night at home alone. Several concerned friends asked, "Will you be OK?"

"I don't know," I replied, "but there is only one way to find out."

"Will you call if you need someone to come?"

"Yes, of course," I replied without thinking. A moment later, I could hear the voice in my head say, *I am not going to call you. I must do this myself.*

For months after my husband's death, I would kiss his pillow, tell him goodnight and tell him that I loved and missed him. After, I would then turn over and cry myself to sleep.

I still miss my husband every day. The passage of time has not changed that for me. I have heard the same thing from widows whose husbands died decades ago. Loss goes with you no matter where you go. You cannot escape its grip.

I have found that often after returning to my home after spending the night with people for several days and then leave, the grief that follows is palpable. Let me give an example. My mother's birthday is May 11. I traveled to her house and we celebrated by eating at her favorite restaurant. Then two days later we had a family celebration at her house. I spent the night and the next morning we attended church together for Mother's Day. As I drove home that evening, I was solemn. The closer I got to my house, the sadder I became. When I was about 15 minutes from home, the tears began. Mom typically requests that I call her after I arrive home. Once inside my house, I called her. Mom (also a widow) said, "I miss you already." I knew immediately what she meant.

"I miss you too," I said. During our brief time together at her house, we had experienced our "used to life," which was filled with conversations, eating meals together, and sharing life with someone we loved. Now, once again, that human connection was gone, and we were back to our new normal—loneliness and sadness.

"It is nice to be missed," I told myself as I hung up the phone.

I found evenings at home especially difficult because they seemed to last forever. I distinctly remember early in my grief journey that I would sit in the living room and keep looking at the clock. Summer nights this loneliness was lessened because I would often sit on the screened porch on the back of the house when I arrived home from work. I would watch and listen to the wildlife. Winter nights were the worst though since porch sitting can't be done in the winter. Even in North Carolina, it's just too cold. The first winter I was trying so hard to find anything to do so that the time before bed would not stand still! You won't believe what saved my sanity. One day I recalled working puzzles when I was a child. My father, sister, and I would sit on the floor in the living room and put together a jigsaw puzzle on top of the coffee table. I knew my mother-in-law had lots of puzzles at her house so I picked up several to take home when I was there for Christmas. It worked wonderfully. Time went by so fast that often I would look at the clock and it would be midnight! Those of you who have worked puzzles know exactly what I am describing. You keep telling yourself, "Let me just find where this piece goes and then I will quit," and on and on you go. I have framed several of the puzzles because the pictures are so beautiful and they also serve as a reminder of the blessing I found in this simple activity.

> Early in my grief journey I would sit in the living room and keep looking at the clock.

During the time when puzzles were such a help, I received the sweetest surprise in the mail from my neighbor's daughter, Heather, whose father had committed suicide. It was a puzzle that she designed. The box that contained the puzzle pieces was all white so I had no idea what the puzzle looked like. I loved that, because it was a challenge as well as a surprise as to what would appear when all the pieces were put in their rightful places! I remember working on it every night for a week. Finished, it was a scene of a curved gravel path surrounded by grass, bushes and trees. Although you could see two curves in the scene, you could not see where the path was going. The words at the top of the puzzle read: *Begin each day as if it were on purpose.* Heather's words touched my heart in a way that only could come from someone who had already taken the path I was traveling. This puzzle was also framed and is hanging on the wall leading to the garage. I look at it often as I leave the house. It is a frequent reminder that I don't know where this journey will take me, but I will start each day on purpose. This puzzle continues to minister to my heart in that I don't know where the path is going but I know the One who does!

M.E. Louis

CHAPTER THREE

HEALING

—◆—

"The LORD is good, a refuge in times of trouble. He cares for those who trust in Him."

Nahum 1:7 (NIV)

I called my pastor several weeks following Bob's death to explain that I wanted to talk with a counselor. He recommended a local Baptist church and added, "If I needed to see a counselor, that is where I would go." That settled it for me so I called and made an appointment. My first meeting was on a Tuesday at 2:00 on September 6, 2013. I wanted to share details that no one else knew about Bob's death with the counselor. I was very nervous and emotional that day. I could only verbalize several sentences at a time before the flood gates opened. I must have used about one half a box of Kleenex that day as I retold the story of Bob's suicide ONE more time. The counselor was also using Kleenex. After I completed my story she said, "Now I know why we were paired together. I haven't experienced a suicide myself, but my husband's best friend hung himself in a park." I had a standing 2:00 appointment every Tuesday from that day until December 13, 2013. I knew this counselor would use the Bible to help me process my anger toward my husband and my anger at God.

Why did the counselor ask me to focus on God's character, God's promises, and to realize there is a purpose in my suffering? She wanted to infuse God right into the middle of my ugly circumstances. She wanted to point me to the God who **"heals the broken-hearted and binds up their wounds." (Psalm 147:3 NIV)**

"You keep track of all my sorrows. You have collected all my tears in Your bottle. You have recorded each one in Your book." (Psalm 56:8 NLT) This verse describes how much God loves and how intimately He cares. Because I cried so much, I would often say to God, "You must have a big bottle!" It was an amazing idea that the God—who created the universe and everything in it—was holding all my tears in a bottle!

The ultimate picture of God's love is evident on the cross, on which God's Son Jesus was crucified to save mankind, for anyone and everyone who believes in Him. If there were any other way to gain access to Heaven, why would He allow His only Son to die on the cross?

"Jesus answered, 'I am the way and the truth and the life. No one comes to the Father except through me.'" (John 14:6 NIV)

As a high school student, I was told that Jesus died on the cross for me and that if I had been the only person on the earth, Jesus still would have gone to the cross... Wow! What AMAZING LOVE! That is when I decided to become a follower of Jesus. Because of His death on the cross, my destiny is sure. When I close my eyes on this earth, I will open them in Heaven...just as my husband did.

"God showed how much He loved us by sending His one and only Son into the world so that we might have eternal life through Him. This is real love—not that we loved God, but that He loved us and sent His Son as a sacrifice to take away our sins." (1 John 4:9-10 NLT)

Focus on God's character

Psalm 139: vs. 1-18 (NLT) reveals a lot about God's character. I have referred to it over and over again throughout my life. My first encounter with this Psalm was in high school when I was struggling with a poor body image. Upon reading verses 13- 15, God gave me a new perspective about my physical appearance. First of all, God made me. He knows me intimately and knows every detail about me with "all the delicate, inner parts of my body." And what God makes is both wonderful and marvelous! Not only that, but verse 15 says that God was there when I was formed in my mother's womb. These facts overwhelmed me with awe in the face of the character of my God.

1. O LORD, you have examined my heart and know everything about me.
2. You know when I sit down or stand up. You know my thoughts even when I am far away.
3. You see me when I travel and when I rest at home. You know everything I do.
4. You know what I am going to say even before I say it, LORD.
5. You go before me and follow me. You place your hand of blessing on my head.
6. Such knowledge it too wonderful for me, too great for me to understand!
7. I can never escape from your Spirit! I can never get away from your presence!
8. If I go up to heaven, you are there; if I go down to the grave, you are there.
9. If I ride the wings of the morning, if I dwell by the farthest oceans,
10. even there your hand will guide me, and your strength will support me.
11. I could ask the darkness to hide me and the light around me to become night
12. but even in darkness I cannot hide from you. To you the night shines as bright as day. Darkness and light are the same to you.

13. You made all the delicate, inner parts of my body and knit me together in my mother's womb.
14. Thank you for making me so wonderfully complex! Your workmanship is marvelous-how well I know it.
15. You watched me as I was being formed in utter seclusion, as I was woven together in the dark of the womb.
16. You saw me before I was born. Every day of my life was recorded in your book. Every moment was laid out before a single day had passed.
17. How precious are your thoughts about me, O God. They cannot be numbered!
18. I can't even count them; they outnumber the grains of sand! And when I wake up, you are still with me.

All these years later as a widow I stand in awe of God because of what else He knows. In Psalm 139 God assures me of the following:

- He knows me, and everything about me (verse 1)
- He knows everything I do (verses 2, 3)
- He knows what I think (verse 2)
- He knows wherever I go as well as everything I do (verse 3)
- He knows what I am going to say before I know it (verse 4)
- He knows where I am and goes ahead of me (verse 5)

- It astonishes me how much he knows about me (verse 6)
- He never leaves me, no matter where I go (verses 7-10, 18)
- He has night vision (verses 11-12)
- He knows when I will die (verse 16)
- He desires a relationship with His creation (verses 17, 18)

These verses were so comforting to me that I made the following entry in my journal:

> *I can leave an authentic mark of gold by trusting God when I encounter difficult circumstances. He will never leave me nor forsake me. He never leaves my side. He is available 24/7 and I can talk to Him about everything and anything. He wants me to come to Him with my doubts, fears, unbelief, etc. Why wouldn't I ask the Creator of the Universe my questions? He knows ALL things because He is God. Thank You that You are an approachable God. You hold my future in Your hands…therefore I will trust in You.*

These verses had a huge mind-altering effect on my life. For someone who had lived as two for so long, it was scary to live alone. Thoughts would race through my mind like, "If I have car trouble, who will I call? If I get sick, who will take me to the doctor? Who will take care of my dog while I am traveling out of town for work?" These and many other questions would paralyze me with fear and cause me to panic. Once I grasped the concept that there was nowhere I could go that God did not see and protect me, I felt a huge sense of relief and peace. Basically, the verses from Psalm 139 tell us, you can't get away from God! He is everywhere! For me, this was very reassuring.

One of the many benefits of marriage is security. As a wife, I knew my husband would take care of me by providing for my physical needs financially. He would also support me emotionally and spiritually. That was a given, which I never gave another thought until my husband died. When I focused on the character of God, I discovered the security for which I longed after my husband's death.

I have discovered a divine truth—a truth that many other people have discovered as well—that God is enough, no matter your circumstance.

"Bad news won't bother them; they have decided to trust the LORD." (Psalm 112:7 CEV)

Focus on God's Promises

"'For I know what I have planned for you', says the LORD. 'I have plans to prosper you, not to harm you. I have plans to give you a future filled with hope.'" (Jeremiah 29:11 NET)

The Bible is full of God's promises. I clung to many of these promises, as I maneuvered one step at a time through my new normal. These promises were a lifeline that God was giving me in my sea of despair.

I wrote about this in another of my many, daily journal entries. **A New Year**

> *Father, many days I feel lost and don't want to face another day of the sameness of unending days that turn into weeks, then months and eventually years. When people were saying, 'Happy New Year,' I was thinking, 'Yippee. I get to live another 365 days without my best friend, supporter and husband.' I know that You have plans for each day and therefore I will trust in You. Whatever the plan is, I know it will be good because You are good. You have tailor made the plans for the rest of my life, so let's do this thing! I love You. Shine through this vessel of Yours.*

The Reality Of Eternity In Heaven

"He has made everything beautiful in its time. He has also set eternity in the human heart; yet no one can fathom what God has done from beginning to end." (Ecclesiastes 3:11 NIV)

When I read this verse, it reminds me that God is in control from the beginning until the end of time and that God makes all things beautiful in His time. I then wrote the following in my journal:

*I have definitely found this verse to be true. You
have used the worst event of my life to show me
Yourself. You have created changes in me, even as I
clung to You with all I had because I had nowhere
else to turn. I knew only You could help me through
this horrific tragedy. ~~Other people may let me down,
but You would not.~~ Thank You for the two blessings You supplied tonight. Help me continue to
take what life I have left holding tightly onto You.
May I only take one day at a time knowing You are
ALREADY THERE.*

The Expectancy Of Heaven

**"He will wipe away every tear from their eyes, and
death shall be no more, neither shall there be mourning, nor crying, nor pain anymore, for the former
things have passed away." (Revelation 21:4 ESV)**

Now that my husband is in Heaven I think a lot
about what he must be experiencing there. I wonder
what it must be like. That is why these verses about
Heaven have such importance to me. I want to know
about Heaven and these verses give me just a glimpse
of what it will be like. I cannot wait to get there!

*The promise of eternity is huge in this widow's jour-
ney. Although this journey has been the hardest
thing I have ever experienced, I know it is so short
compared to the eternity of Heaven. I will face each
new day knowing it brings me closer to Christ's*

return. I will call You for help, strength and guidance daily. One day there will be NO MORE pain, sorrow, or mourning!!!! What a day that will be!

Then, a few days later, I wrote the following in my journal:

Comfort comes from being known by the God who knows all. Nothing takes Him by surprise or scares Him. He can handle anything and everything that happens in the world. I am comforted by the knowledge that Heaven exists and that when I die I will be there... a place with no sorrow, pain, suffering, doubt, fear, anxiousness, or guilt. I can only imagine what Heaven will be like... and I can't wait to see God face-to-face and spend eternity with Him! same girl

"And those who know Your name will put their trust in You, for You, O LORD, have not forsaken those who seek You." (Psalm 9:10 NASB)

While I am still on planet Earth I will trust God. The desire to trust God doesn't erase my sadness or my fear about the future. It is a decision I have to make each and every day. It does not come naturally and often is very hard. Will I trust God even as my life feels shortened by sadness? Will I surrender my future into the loving hands of God?

God has used scripture to bring comfort, truth and unexplainable joy into my life. This book contains many of the verses that brought healing to my broken heart. Reading the Bible refocused my mind on the truth about God rather than letting emotions dictate my actions. Not only was I reading the Bible daily but I had posted Bible verses all over my house upstairs and down. For example, on the microwave, the back door that leads into the garage, the window over the kitchen sink, the mirror in the bathroom, on the steering wheel of the car, etc. You get the idea! You will find some of the verses that impacted my life in the back of the book. I invite you to cut them out and post them where they will be seen. In addition, I have found that listening to Christian music can help by interrupting my thoughts and redirecting my mind to God's love and trustworthiness.

God In The Details

"The LORD directs the steps of the godly. He delights in every detail of their lives. Though they stumble, they will never fall, for the LORD holds them by the hand." (Psalm 37:23-24 NLT)

I have experienced God taking me by the hand. Often, He just holds my hand to reassure me that He loves me. Other times, He uses His Holy Spirit within me to tell me something and to give me instruction on what to do in a particular situation. God is all about details—just look at the beauty of creation! Take a moment to ponder the divine details of nature and all of God's creatures. Consider the complexity of the human body. My personal favorite is looking at the stars. Though they are too numerous to count, God knows each of the stars by name! Of course He does because He made each of them. **"He determines the number of stars and calls them by name." (Psalm 147:4 NIV)**

God Keeps His Word

God promises in **Hebrews 13:5** that, **"I will never desert you, nor will I ever forsake you." (NAS)** God is trustworthy. He is unable to lie, therefore He keeps all of His promises.

I can take God at His word, just as Abraham did—no matter how impossible that might seem...like having a baby, your first baby at 100 years old!

In this pivotal Old Testament event, God promised Abraham that he and his wife would bear a son. Further, God promised him that through his son He would make Abraham the father of a multitude of nations. As he heard this promise, Abraham laughed. His wife Sarah later had the same response for in reality both were very old, far beyond child-bearing years. Yet just as promised, Sarah did indeed conceive and give birth to Isaac, Abraham's heir. Through Isaac, Abraham became the patriarch of God's chosen people Israel. God always keeps His promises!

Check out the unbelievable story in **Genesis 17:15-17; Genesis 18:9-14; Genesis 21:1-7.**

I have seen God's provision over and over again on this journey. Sometimes it is huge; other times it is small, even intimate. Either way, it is always obvious that it is God's activity.

Many nights when I am afraid, stressed, over-whelmed, lonely or sad, I pray to Him. In the dead stillness of the night I know He's awake because He never sleeps, so I talk to Him about my concerns. Then I close my eyes and sleep because I have given everything over to Him "to handle". The next day I look for His activity and I see it! I cannot imagine walking this most difficult journey without My Heavenly Father holding me.

It is amazing to me that the God of the Universe is so interested in my life! May I never get over this amazing love or take it for granted. God wants to use me to accomplish His purposes. He desires a relationship with His creation. That concept just blows my mind!

CHAPTER FOUR

GOD STORIES

$\diamond$

*"In the morning, LORD, you hear my voice;
in the morning I lay my requests before you and
wait expectantly."*

Psalm 5:3

I have learned to take one step at a time, one day at a time. God knows all, so He knows what each day presents. I have found that as I focus on Him during each day rather than on my tasks, my to do list, or my circumstances, He will either take care of the issues or take care of me through them. This life lesson has been learned since my husband's death, little by little, baby step by baby step.

As I have learned to let go, I see Him more clearly and more frequently. So much so that many days I look forward with expectation to see how He will act…and act He does. This may not happen to everyone but the following are stories of God's activity.

Faithful in the Storm

Mom and I were vacationing at North Myrtle Beach the week of September 28, 2015. We were keeping an eye on the weather forecast because Hurricane Joaquin was off the coast. On Friday, October 1, the forecast for Joaquin was that it would stay away from the South Carolina coast and Myrtle Beach would get one to five inches of rain. Since the forecast was just rain, we decided to head out for the afternoon. We did some shopping, ate lunch and saw a movie. While in the theatre, we heard the rain pounding on the roof. As we drove back to the condo, the outer lanes of Highway 17 were flooded, but the inner lanes were good. We had planned to eat dinner at Hoskins, but when we arrived they were closed. As we approached Ocean Boulevard it was blocked off with barricades. Our condo was one mile down Ocean Boulevard. I decided to drive several blocks down the road that paralleled Ocean Boulevard, and then head towards Ocean Boulevard. Once there, I turned left onto Ocean Boulevard or I should say "Lake Boulevard" and it was dark! We drove several blocks and then the car's engine sounded like it was going to stall, and I was afraid to continue knowing we could become stranded in the water. I decided to pull into a driveway, walked up the stairs to the front door of the house and rang the doorbell. I remember thinking, "It is 7:00 at night. They are not going to answer the door." I was relieved when a lady and a man answered the door. I explained the situation to them and they called 911. The response from 911 was that they had so many calls that they would only come if we were stranded. The man and woman insisted that I pull the car into the carport and spend the night with them! The house was huge and there were five middle aged couples staying for two weeks. They were all from Virginia. They asked if we had eaten dinner to which we responded, "No." They began to pull out all kinds of food and placed it on the big dining room table in the kitchen: corned beef, cabbage, pinto beans, homemade biscuits (who makes homemade biscuits anymore?), macadamia cookies, and chocolate pound cake. The four women sat around the table with my mom and I and talked

> We were only a half mile from our condo that night, but we would have never made it.

and showed us pictures of their grandchildren. The men watched football on television. We learned that this group gets together at this same time every year. They all come to North Myrtle Beach and stay for two weeks. One of the couples had left earlier that day, so there was an empty bedroom on the second floor that contained two single beds. They presented Mom and I with pajamas, toothbrushes and toothpaste. The next day, the men were cooking breakfast and fed us again. We were only a half mile from our condo that night, but we would have never made it. As we drove to the condo after breakfast, we passed cars in the middle of Ocean Boulevard that had been abandoned and were flooded. Owners were trying to salvage items from their cars. This could have been us. What a story of God's provision. You cannot make this stuff up!

Unexpected Headlines

My husband and I met at the University of North Carolina in Chapel Hill and were huge sports fans. We had season tickets to the basketball games. After he died, I relinquished my tickets. When a legendary coach of the Tar Heels, Dean Smith died, a public service to remember him was planned. I knew that if my husband were alive, there would be no way he would miss this service. I invited my mom and one of her friends to join me.

When my husband and I had attended the games, our seats were always in the nosebleed section. I decided that since my "seat mate" was missing, the three of us would sit in our game seats way up high, in memory of him. Needless to say, we stuck out because the first floor of the arena was not full. Unbeknownst to us, there was a newspaper reporter also sitting in the upper deck. He approached us and asked, "Why are you sitting way up here?" He interviewed us and took notes. Never did I expect the story I told him about my husband to appear in the paper. Here is an excerpt from *The Fayetteville Observer* article written by Stephen Scramm entitled *Dean Smith's Tar Heel family bids farewell from their seats in the sky*, (February 2, 2015).

> *Nearly an hour before Sunday's memorial service for Dean Smith, only three of the seats in Section 228 were taken. Stuart, Ellyn and M.E. had claimed three seats in Row K. When M.E. heard that there would be a public service for Coach Dean Smith, who died Feb. 7 at the age of 83, M.E. knew exactly where she would be. Her husband died in August. Row K, Seat 1 was his piece of Blue Heaven. He would have wanted her there. 'He gets to welcome Dean Smith into heaven,' she said. 'How awesome is that?'*

You most definitely cannot make this stuff up!

Up, Up, And Away

For the first time ever the Freedom Hot Air Balloon Fest was held in my hometown! It is usually held in a town about thirty minutes away, but this year it was moved. One of my close friends, TJ, was volunteering at the event and her job was to work with the balloon pilots. She became acquainted with one of them, and told me he was interested in taking me up, up and away! What an experience. The ride lasted an hour and it was the most serene trip just above the treetops. People ran out of their houses to wave at us. It was so calm and relaxing—everything I thought it would be and much more.

Only My Heavenly Father would know the significance of this trip to the sky. First, the ride happened three days after what would have been my 36th wedding anniversary. Second, my husband had planned a surprise hot air balloon ride for our 33rd anniversary. Unfortunately, due to weather, the event was cancelled three times. We never got to take our romantic hot air balloon trip. Now, three years and three days later, came this belated anniversary gift. Thank you, God.

You can't make this stuff up!

Humbling Reality Check

While driving to Virginia, I passed a couple with two dogs at an intersection holding up a sign that said "Need Help." I drove past them, but later felt God's Holy Spirit nudging me to provide food for the dogs. I drove another two blocks and discovered a Walmart, so I purchased the dog food and headed back to the intersection where the couple was. When I arrived, I asked the man to remove the dog food from the back seat of my car. He said, "Thank you" and explained that his wife had just started a job at a local restaurant as a waitress!

He then asked, "Can she use your phone to make a call?"

I thought to myself, *No...that wasn't part of the bargain. I am giving what I want to give and nothing more.*

Then it dawned on me. What a gift! I have the opportunity to share in the excitement and good news of two complete strangers. God taught me that often helping others requires sacrifice. In my case, I needed to sacrifice my selfishness.

Explain This

One day, a stray dog wandered into my neighborhood and lay down on the front porch of my neighbor's house. A neighbor and I approached the dog, an older female Labrador. She was very docile and wearing a chip tag on her collar. I called the phone number on the tag and left my information on the answering machine at 4:30 p.m. I prayed to God, asking that the staff at Animal Control would be expedient in uniting the dog with its family. I was sure they were worried about their pet. The owner called at 7:00 p.m. and came to pick up his dog. I thanked God for answering my prayer so quickly.

When he arrived, the owner explained that he had called Animal Control at 4:15 p.m., after realizing his dog had gone missing. Our calls were only 15 minutes apart. *This could only be God's divine timing*, I thought to myself. The next day, a man from Animal Control called and said he was returning my call from yesterday. I explained that the dog and its owner had already been reunited. "That's strange," he replied, "because the phone only rings at my desk and I was off yesterday."

You can't make this stuff up!

Not Just A Coincidence

Today I had a massage appointment with Barbra. I brought a grief book for Barbra to pass onto a friend of hers whose mother had recently become a widow. When I presented the book to Barbra, she said, "You're not going to believe this, but my friend is in the room next door. She just finished having a massage. I am going to give it to her now!"

CHAPTER FIVE

THRIVING

"Consider it a sheer gift, friends, when tests and challenges come at you from all sides. You know that under pressure, your faith-life is forced into the open and shows its true colors. So don't try to get out of anything prematurely. Let it do its work so you become mature and well-developed, not deficient in any way."

James 1:2–4 (MSG)

I have learned many things the past 5 years. I have chartered many unknown waters. I have gone from wishing and praying that God would end my life to waiting with anticipation where God wants me to go from here. Only the work of God in my life could accomplish such a dramatic shift. When God says over and over again in His Word that He will take care of widows He means it. I have seen God's activity and felt His presence in my life like I've never seen before. I want Him to get the glory for everything that comes from this tragedy.

Difficult circumstances are inevitable in life. How we respond to them will make us either bitter or better. I have found that suffering has deepened my relationship with God. If I were to sum up in one sentence what I have learned since August 7, 2013 it would be that through suffering God makes His presence known. In life we will experience difficult things. We may not be able to do anything about the circumstance we find ourselves in, but we can do something about how we handle ourselves as we go through it. In *Fingerprints of God (Session 6)* Jennifer Rothschild makes a great point when she says, "Don't let your difficult circumstance define you. Let it refine you."

As well as Elisabeth Elliot in her book, THE PATH OF LONELINESS, (2001) states, "Nothing takes Him by surprise. But nothing is for nothing, either. His plan is to make me holy, and hardship is indispensable for that as long as we live in this hard old world. All I have to do is accept it."

Looking Back at How Far I Have Come

On January 1, 2016, I faced the beginning of a new year alone. It was a very difficult day for me, and I wrote in my journal:

*I received a text message from Peggy today:
"HAPPY NEW YEAR. I pray that 2016 will hold
much comfort, joy and happiness for you. And that
you can finish your office and maybe get your hot air
balloon ride! Love you girlfriend!"*

*The thought and reality of spending another entire
year without my husband is overwhelming. It is an
exhausting thought. I am very sad today and have
little energy to accomplish anything, although I
have the next three days off from work!*

*In the meantime, I'm trusting the One who knows
the plan and my future. I love you, O LORD, my
strength.*

It is interesting to look back and see how far I have
come since this journal entry. I did ride in a hot air
balloon and am in the process of finishing my office.
When I wrote this, I never thought those things were
possible.

**"Ah, LORD GOD! It is You who have made the
heavens and the earth by Your great power and by
Your outstretched arm! Nothing is too hard for
You." (Jeremiah 32:17 ESV)**

How I Have Been Restored and Changed

"He restores my strength. He leads me down the right paths for the sake of His reputation." (Psalm 23:3 NET)

The biblical meaning of the word "restores" is to receive back more than has been lost to the point where the final state is greater than the original condition. This definition describes well what I have experienced over the past five years. God used my husband's suicide to not only change my life, but to create a better me.

Now, making time to read the Bible, journal and pray each day is a priority. I talk with Him throughout the day about my concerns, fears, decisions and needs. This simple act lets me release my worries and hand them over to God. He is big enough to handle them. I pray more readily and more often.

"Let the morning bring me word of Your unfailing love, for I have put my trust in You. Show me the way I should go, for to You I entrust my life." (Psalm 143: 8 NIV)

When I focus on how much God loves me, I can entrust Him with my life. I love that this is a conditional statement. When I read about Your unfailing love, then it produces trust in You. In other words, you cannot have one without the other.

I also more quickly and clearly see the blessings in my life. As I have described previously, I watch for His activity. I have found that this journey has increased my love for Jesus such that I often shed tears when I read the Bible or pray. His relationship with me is so precious now that I have a gratefulness I have never before experienced.

Another change I notice is that community has become more important to me than ever before. I discovered that I had more friends than I knew I had. It has been amazing to see how God has enlarged my community. He has transformed some of my friends into family. I have become more intentional in my relationships, making sure I verbalize my love to others. I want them to know how important they are and how glad I am that they are a part of my life. People never know what they mean to you unless you say it. Say and show love often to the important people in your life.

> I discovered I had more friends than I knew I had.

Of the three main changes in my life, community has been the most transforming. This tragedy not only brought me out of my shell, it helped me to blossom as well. Webster's Dictionary defines the word "blossom" as follows: "To flourish and prosper." Today, I am flourishing and prospering where I have been planted.

Ferree Hardy in her book, *Postcards from the Widows' Path*, (2012), expressed it this way, "We never know what cast of characters God will call into our lives; we only know that they will be called and that our lives will be woven together in ways we would never imagined."

What Changes Others See in Me

As I attempted to articulate to a friend how I was not the same person I was prior to my husband's death, I used the story of Moses coming down the mountain after receiving the Ten Commandments from God. "Others can't see the change," I told my friend, "but my inside is shining."

"Oh, I can see it," she responded.

I have changed dramatically since Bob's death and I was curious if others had noticed this change. So I asked friends that know me well to describe what, if any, changes they have seen in me since my husband's death. It was amazing to read their comments because they helped to confirm the changes that have taken place. The following are their comments.

"I can't imagine what you have walked through on your pilgrim journey these few years. It has taken courage to move forward. That is an area of growth. You are more courageous than before. You have taken big steps of faith. You have done things that took courage to do on your own, i.e. the balloon ride. I think the word courage is my main word for you... courage to move forward, courage to reach out to other widows when you are grieving, courage to believe God and see Him in all the details of your life, and courage to share your story in a book. You have stepped out of your comfort zone." —*Teresa*

"M.E. has spiritually grown and changed over the last five years due to the unexpected death of her best friend and beloved husband. A woman who suffered so greatly and yet, she moves onward depending on God's grace and love to guide her on this journey

> "One word comes to mind when I think of M.E. and that is 'courageous.'"

of life. She is a Christian role model and a very strong woman, even though at times she cannot see it herself and God has given her a heart of compassion to minister to those individuals that have lost a loved one, especially to widows. One word comes to mind when I think of her and that is 'courageous.'" —*Kelly*

"To say that the unexpected absence of M.E.'s husband changed lives is an understatement. I had the unique privilege of walking alongside M.E. after Bob's death and witnessed the depth of her love for him in a unique way as she journeyed through excruciating grief. I had always admired their comradery—something rarely displayed among married couples. Their shared passion for things that seemed common to other people was evidence of their partnership. Take gardening, for example; who else updates a growth chart daily for the quantity of squash and cucumbers grown in a season? The trauma of losing Bob forced M.E. into a natural cocoon of sorts—for protection, growth and healing. During that time God surrounded her with people, His Word and His Presence. M.E. spent significant amounts of time seeking God, meaning, healing and purpose. An introverted woman who perceived herself as only being accepted because she was Pastor Bob's wife emerged as a beautiful woman radiating courage, confidence and Jesus. Her pain has been transformed into scars that God is using to comfort and shape women. She has begun a new growing season. Her garden is nurtured year round as she plants words of encouragement for widows, fertilizing them with God's Word, shares tears of sadness and joy along each row, and harvests an abundance of peace as changed lives emerge." —*TJ*

Tate's Garden 2009

My nickname is Boo.

Boo ain't much on the hoeing part, and she's about half-'n-half on the planting part, but she sure is something on the picking and eating part!

DATE	CUCUMBERS	SQUASH	TOMATOES	PEPPERS
6-15-09		1		
6-20-09	8	45		
6-21-09	3			
6-22-09		5		
6-23-09	12	6		
6-24-09	6	6		
6-27-09	18	Replanted		1
6-28-09	3			
6-30-09	13			2
7-02-09	6			
7-04-09	3			
7-07-09	12			
7-09-09	10			
7-11-09	4		3	12
7-16-09	5		2	
7-18-09	2			28
7-20-09	2		3	
7-28-09	9			67
8-01-09			2=10	37
8-04-09				60
8-08-09		2		27
8-10-09	2			
8-13-09	2=120	1=66		68
8-16-09				48
8-30-09				48
9-05-09				69
9-15-09				175
9-17-09				144

9-26-09				262
10-03-09				91
10-04-09				10
10-11-09				138
10-20-09				42
11-06-09				75
11-22-09				149
11-28-09				73
12-12-09				39=1665

"I met M. E. in the fall of 2005 when we became neighbors. She and Bob were already living in the neighborhood. The day we met I talked more with Bob than M. E. She was polite, but quiet and reserved. That didn't stop me from attending her neighborhood Bible study. It was there in her home that I found M.E. to be hospitable. She was a strong Christian and led our Bible studies. Her understanding of the Bible was apparent. M. E. was a godly Pastor's wife. Her daily walk and personal relationship with God was to be admired. When Bob died, I thought M. E. would sell her home and move in with her mother, also a widow. To my surprise M. E. did the opposite. She not only stayed in her home, but she made plans to have a garage built. She also repainted, and renovated Bob's closet into her prayer room and added to her outside landscaping. She quickly began adapting to her 'new normal' as she called it. Throughout those projects God resonated in M. E.'s life. She saw

His hand in the details and shared openly. At the first anniversary of Bob's death M. E. had an open house. She posted notes and signs inside and out. The postings detailed what she saw and experienced God do in that year. M. E., the quiet, reserved introvert found a new purpose. She desired to be a comforter to widows. In God's timing He allowed her opportunity after opportunity to do just that. Not only did M.E. feel led to write this book, but she also felt led to lead a widows Bible study in her home. God used M. E. and her hospitable nature to nurture. To say M. E. came out of her shell is too bold. Instead, I like to think that her voice was no longer a whisper. M. E. learned that people valued her thoughts and opinions just as much as they once did Bob's. Genesis 2:24 states, '… and they shall become one flesh.' That was true of Bob and M. E. I saw and continue to see Bob's legacy living on through his soul mate, M.E." —*Gayle*

"My friend, M. E., since I have known her, has always had a sweet dedicated walk with God leading a neighborhood Bible Study and loving the youth at church. But the day M. E.'s husband died, God did an amazing work in and through her life. On that day, she let the enemy Satan know she was standing her ground and would not let him win through this tragedy. God gave her the strength, resolve and a brave courage to stand up for her faith in God through tragedy. She was tested on that day and she stood her ground like Job. 'Blessed be the name of the Lord.' And it continued to grow as she poured out her heart to God and others. There was a firm faith like Abraham waiting for God's plan and David grieving running and hiding in caves – an 'I won't give up' faith. She devoured God's Word as never before and was firm in her standing on God's side. M. E.'s foundation in God's Word and trust in Him helped her get through the depression, fear and grief. She became more outgoing than before, leaning on God's strength and opened up to others to sharing with them what God had done like writing this book. A true boldness! Before when Bob was alive, he was more the outspoken minister of the gospel, but now God has given M. E. that gift. She is now leading in that role. I love my honest conversations with M. E. about God, pain, healing and God's Word that is so fresh in her heart. Daily she looks for touch's of God in her life, knowing His presence is there and can't wait to share what God is doing. She is bringing glory to God in a new way as she can't wait to share with others what God is doing. But she has also become an even greater listener, "bearing one another's burdens" in people's lives, especially other widows and those who have had losses in their lives." —*Vonnie*

> "M.E.'s foundation in God's Word and trust in Him helped her get through the depression, fear and grief."

"M.E. and I first met a number of years ago when she co-led a women's Bible study at our church in which I participated. Our friendship really began in earnest, however, after her husband died. I, too, had been widowed, and took the opportunity to reach out to M.E. with the Love of Christ, which had become so clear during my own grief years before. Over the course of three years since, we have become fast friends, spending untold sweet hours rocking on the porch talking about things of the Lord. Having walked through unspeakable tragedy and grief, my friend is now best defined by the bubbling-over, can't-wait-to-tell-you-about-it Glory and Goodness of God! I knew her before to be a committed Christian who loved her Savior. However, I have witnessed first-hand God's transformational power in her heart and life. These days, you simply can't be around M.E. without hearing about the God she loves; this God who continues to faithfully carry her through darkness to a place of new joy and purpose. You cannot be around M.E. without seeing the love of Christ shining in her countenance. God's love and goodness in her widowhood has been a beautiful thing to witness. To Him be all praise and glory. Psalm 71 speaks so clearly of M.E.: 'For you have been my hope, Sovereign LORD, my confidence since my youth. From birth I have relied on you; you brought me forth from my mother's womb. I will ever praise you. I have become a sign to many; you are my strong refuge. My mouth is filled with your praise, declaring your splendor all day long.' (Psalm 71: 5-8 NIV)" — *Terri*

CHAPTER SIX

CHANGE AND PURPOSE

"Blessed be the God, and Father of our Lord Jesus Christ, the Father of mercies and God of all comfort; who comforts us in all our affliction so we may be able to comfort those who are in any affliction with the comfort with which we ourselves are comforted by God."

2 Corinthians 1:3, 4 (NAS)

My new normal has created ministry opportunities. I now have the privilege of walking beside widows who are experiencing the same despair I experienced.

When I meet a widow, we automatically connect because we share a tremendous sense of loss. The connection provides a bond that is unique to widows. This is the way that God designed comfort. God comforts us and He uses what we have learned to comfort someone else. The word "comfort" means to come forth with strength. Therefore, when we offer comfort to another person, we are enabling them to come forth with strength so that they can take the next step. This is one way that suffering added purpose to my life.

Although this concept was the most difficult one for me to comprehend and accept, I now understand and embrace it. It helps to not only have a sense of purpose as a result of my excruciating pain and grief, but to know that God experientially qualified me to comfort others with the comfort I received from Him.

P – Planned
U – Use to
R – Relate by
P – Providing
O – Others and ourselves
S – Something
E - Extraordinary

This acrostic for purpose describes what I have experienced. Having a purpose is life giving to the one who offers the comfort as well as to the one who receives it. Purpose is planned by God. He wants us to use what we have learned to pass it on to someone else. This offers others and ourselves something extraordinary; being a part of God's activity and His plan for our lives. It is wonderful to have a purpose in these years following something so horrible!

God used the timely sermon below to speak to me about my next season of life, and how He wants to use me in a new ministry.

Excerpt from Doug Humphrey's sermon, Senior Pastor of Triangle Community Church, taken from Judges 6 and 7 entitled, *Gideon: An Unlikely Hero - Part 4 of Judges.* "When God wants to accomplish something extraordinary, what kind of a person does he normally use? God uses ordinary people to accomplish extraordinary tasks. God approached Gideon about becoming a warrior and becoming a leader of the Israelite army to defeat the Midianites. Gideon was a fearful man – but God looks at us as what we can be, not for what we are. Gideon began to make excuses as to why he wasn't a good candidate for the job. God's response: 'Have I not sent you? Surely, I will be with you.' What else do we need to know? We have no excuse for what God has asked us to do. If God has called you to do something, it doesn't matter what the odds are from a human perspective. No challenge is too great for God. In fact, God loves to put us in situations where we are in way over our heads. That way, when God pulls it off, He gets the glory. Gideon knew that God was the hero of this story. Gideon was just the human instrument God used to accomplish His purposes."

> "God looks at us for what we can be, not for what we are."

I can relate to Gideon. I am an introvert who prefers to stay out of the spotlight—unlike my husband, who preached in churches for 28 years and was often in the spotlight. Bob was gifted with a strong commanding voice. When he preached, people listened. In describing Bob's voice, Pastor Doug used to say, "I could listen to Pastor Bob read the telephone book!"

When God began prompting me to start writing a book, I thought, *You have got the wrong person. I don't know how to write a book!* This was quickly followed by what am I saying? I just told the One who made me what I could and couldn't do! Talk about odds… God must like it when the odds are an overwhelming long shot! As was the case with Gideon, I am the instrument God has used to write this book and He will use it for His purpose. On this long and painful journey, I have found one overarching truth: God is enough. I have something in common with Gideon. I know that God is the hero of my story, too.

After working on the book for one month and reflecting on what I had learned three years following Bob's death, I wrote this entry in my journal:

Father, I cannot fathom what this journey would be like without You. The journey has been treacherous, steep, lonely, emotionally draining, unfamiliar, scary and intimidating. But what I have learned on it is priceless. I have deepened my relationship with You as well as with others. I also have learned many things about myself. Thank You that now I am able to rejoin life hand in hand with You. May I never forget what I have learned on this arduous journey! May I take what I've learned to others! All the while may I praise my Savior...for He has done great things! God will continually work in our lives for His goal is to make us look more and more like His Son. May we never cease to see His activity in our lives.

"To all who mourn… He will give beauty for ashes; joy instead of mourning; praise instead of heaviness. For God has planted them like strong and graceful oaks for His own glory." (Isaiah 61:3 TLB)

New Found Joy

God has mended this broken vessel piece by piece. It has been a painful, long journey. He has turned my mourning into dancing! Only God could have accomplished this. The scars that remain serve to remind me of what God has done and how faithful He has been. He has lifted me out of a cavernous pit onto solid ground. Only a loving God would invest that much time on mending me mentally, physically, and spiritually. He loved me to death (the death of His only Son, Jesus). I can trust Him with the rest of my life and for the rest of my life. He will continue His work in me.

Sharon Earnest, also a widow, stated succinctly in her book, *Suffering Is My Friend & Not My Enemy*, (2012) what I have learned about God through suffering. God's word has become my source of strength and my guide book.

> *"Jesus tells us that without Him we can do nothing. In the midst of suffering we find ourselves vulnerable, weak, cast down, and dependent. In the world's eye this is a catastrophe, but in the eyes of the Lord this is good. He is training us to depend upon Him and Him alone. I have certainly found this to be true in my life. It seems that I keep learning this lesson at a deeper level each time I face adversity. In the days ahead we can no longer depend upon our thoughts, ideas and wisdom. We need to hear from the Lord. We need His wisdom. We need His guidance. As Johannes Fascius said, 'The only way to go through tribulations is to have an ear to hear what the Lord is saying and then to obey His word.' One thing is certain; we are more inclined to cry out to God and wait for a word from Him when we are suffering. This is His way of disciplining us so that living by His word becomes a way of life."*

Moving On

This part of my life's story began with my husband's suicide. However, my story is far from over. I am still here. As long as I have breath, God is not finished with me. He is the one who wrote this story and He will continue to do so.

Your story is not over either, even if the pain you are experiencing makes it feel as if it is. If you are still breathing, God WILL work all things for your GOOD and His Glory. We all have a story of the good, the bad and the ugly. God is right in the middle of that story—all we have to do is look for Him. He is *always* there. Talk to God and ask Him to show Himself. He loves to answer that request. Go for it! What do you have to lose?

"If you seek Him, He will let you find Him." (1 Chronicles 28: 9 NASB)

I thought it very fitting to end by leaving a "food for thought" that was taped to the inside cover of my husband's bible. **When the Pathway seems darkest and life's storms are all around, that's when the Lord sends a miracle, moves the mountains, calms the sea. He gives us strength for every need, and I know He will be there for us today and tomorrow and always:** *Fear not, for I am with you… I will strengthen you… I will help you….*" **(Isaiah 41:10)**

M.E. Louis

CHAPTER SEVEN

PROVIDING COMFORT DO AND DON'TS

◆

My desire is to use my experience with grief to share those resources and practices that helped me after the loss of my beloved husband. Equally, I want others to understand those things that do not help someone experiencing grief.

Behaviors That Provide Comfort

"When Job's three friends, Eliphaz the Temanite, Bildad the Shuhite, and Zophar the Naamathite, heard about all the troubles that had come upon him, they set out from their homes and met together by agreement to go and sympathize with him and comfort him. Then they sat on the ground with him for seven days and seven nights. No one

said a word to him, because they saw how great his suffering was." (Job 2:11, 13 NIV)

I have included these verses from Job, not because we need to stay a week with someone who is suffering, but rather to see the insight of Job's friends. They said nothing because they saw "how great his suffering was." This is a good rule of thumb when trying to provide comfort to someone who is grieving. Your presence is more important than your words. Here are things that offered comfort to me:

- Hugs.
- A person's presence without words or very few words.
- Phone calls, text messages as well as emails expressing sympathy and love. Sharing stories about the deceased helps the family remember the good times. If you have a story to tell about the deceased, share it. Although it will more than likely bring tears to the bereaved, it will be a treasure to them, because it keeps the person's memory alive.
- Cards that contain personal written messages.
- Meeting practical needs of the person in grief— meals, yard work, answering the phone, grocery shopping, spending the night with the survivor, taking care of children, etc.
- Offering to do something specific. For example, saying to the bereaved: "I would like to bring you dinner this week. What night would be

good for you?" "I am going to the grocery store, what may I pick up for you?" "While I am here, can I help you do anything?"

- If a family member wants to tell a story about their loved one, take time to listen. You have no idea how much that means to someone who is grieving.

- Sending cards on significant dates of the lost loved one—for example a wedding anniversary, or birthday or the date of the beloved one's death.

Behaviors That Did Not Provide Comfort

"When there are many words, transgression is unavoidable, but he who restrains his lips is wise." (Proverbs 10:19 NASB)

This verse gives a good rule of thumb when talking with those grieving. People are uncomfortable when they see family members or friends in pain. They wish to say something to lighten their grief. That "something" doesn't exist. I realize that people are uncomfortable with death and don't know what to say to those grieving. Shortly after Bob's death one of my friends called and said, "M.E. I don't know what to say." That statement provided much comfort because he spoke the truth and did not add anything to try and make me feel better.

These are behaviors that do not help those in pain deal with their grief:

- Saying things like: "He's is in a better place" or "God needed him more than we did" "Be strong. You need to be strong."

Gayle Roper in her book, *A Widow's Journey,* (2016) wrote "People say things with good intent. I know that. Still they hurt. 'All things work for good. God only takes the good ones. God is in control.' Any my favorite wrong thing: 'Isn't it wonderful that he's in heaven with the Lord?' Quite frankly, it isn't wonderful. He should be here with me."

- Lack of follow through is also difficult for those in grief to process. For example, if a friend says, "I will call you next week about getting together." Then, no phone call follows, .
- Open ended questions like "How are you?" or "What can I do for you?" are not easy for grief-stricken people to answer. They are in a fog and are attempting to survive each day, one hour at a time.
- Lack of mentioning the deceased in the presence of the family. Saying nothing is interpreted by survivors that you have forgotten their loved one. God gave us tears for healing, so don't let the possibility of tears deter you from talking about the deceased. In sharing stories about the person lost, you soothe a family member's soul and minister in ways you will never fully understand.

ABOUT THE AUTHOR

M. E. Louis is a native of North Carolina and grew up in Chapel Hill. She attended the University of North Carolina at Chapel Hill where she met the love of her life during her freshman year. They married four years later. M. E. Louis was married to her pastor husband Bob for 33 years until he chose to end his life on August 7, 2013. She describes the graphic details of his death with all the intense emotions that surrounded her discovery that tragic morning. She honestly and openly describes her struggles as well as her new found realization that God is enough. M. E. Louis lives in N.C. and loves doing anything outdoors, especially working in her yard.

If you would like to contact M.E.Louis, please feel free to email me at: m.e.louis8713@gmail.com.

CLOSING THOUGHTS

I cannot write this book without including an opportunity for those who don't know what Jesus did for them, to learn about God's plan of salvation and about the only way to eternal life. Jesus said, **"I am the resurrection and the life. The person who believes in Me, even if he dies, will live." (John 11:25)** Someone once said, "Death is only one heartbeat away." But the Christ follower has assurance that there is life beyond this one, eternal life with God, that begins the moment a person puts their faith in Jesus. Why did Jesus willingly die on the cross if there was any other way to Heaven?

God's Love, Grace and Plan of Salvation - Command Evangelism, Inc.

In 2 Timothy 1:9-10 the apostle Paul was telling young Timothy about God's gift of grace through Jesus Christ.

"(God) who has saved us, and called us with a holy calling, not according to our works, but according to His own purpose and grace which was granted us in Christ Jesus from all eternity, but now has been revealed by the appearing of our Savior Jesus Christ, who abolished death, and brought life and immortality to light through the <u>gospel</u>." (NAS)

What is the <u>GOSPEL</u>? It is good news! That God sent His son Jesus Christ to die on the cross for our sins that we may be right with God the Father. Jesus removed our sin! He set us free! His resurrection shows God's acceptance of His death on the cross.

All we have to do to be saved is to <u>BELIEVE</u> that what Jesus Christ did on the cross was to save us. Now believe that!! The jailer in Acts 16 asked Paul, "What must I <u>DO</u> to be saved?" The apostle Paul said, "Believe on the Lord Jesus Christ and <u>you will be saved</u>."

God planned our salvation in eternity past. God has already forgiven us through Jesus Christ! All we have to do is to BELIEVE the gospel that Jesus Christ died for our sins, He was buried for our sins, He arose from the dead on the third day.

BECAUSE GOD LOVES YOU, He gave His only begotten son (Jesus) to die on the cross for your sins. No matter how bad your sins are or have been <u>they have already been</u> forgiven. I ask you <u>now</u> at this moment to <u>BELIEVE</u> the gospel and receive God's gift of salvation.

You can say the following to God:

"Lord Jesus, thank you for giving your life for my sins. I believe in you and accept your payment on the cross for my sins. I ask you to take control of my life. I want to trust you for the rest of my life."

I would encourage you to tell someone if you made the decision to become a Jesus follower. Live every day <u>enjoying God's grace given to you</u> through His Son, Jesus Christ!

M.E. Louis

LIST OF BOOKS TO HELP COPE WITH GRIEF

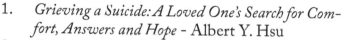

1. *Grieving a Suicide: A Loved One's Search for Comfort, Answers and Hope* - Albert Y. Hsu
2. *Experiencing Grief* - H. Norman Wright
3. *The Path Of Loneliness* - Elisabeth Elliot
4. *Grieving a Suicide: Help for the Aftershock* - David Powlison
5. *Finding Your Way after the Suicide of Someone You Love* - David B. Biebel & Suzanne L. Foster
6. *Becoming A Widow: The Ache of Missing Your Other Half* - Elizabeth W.D. Groves
7. *Hope after Suicide: One Woman's Journey from Darkness to Light* - Wendy Parmley
8. *After Suicide: A Ray of Hope for Those Left Behind* - E. Betsy Ross
9. *Silent Grief: Living in the Wake of a Suicide Revised Edition* - Christopher Lukas
10. *Healing After the Suicide of a Loved One* - Ann Smolin

11. *After Suicide Loss: Coping with Your Grief, 2nd Edition* - Jack Jordan
12. *Making Peace with Suicide: A Book of Hope, Understanding and Comfort* - Adele Ryan McDowell
13. *The Gift of Second: Healing from the Impact of Suicide* - Brandy Liebeck
14. *Finding Peace without all the Pieces: After a Loved One's Suicide* - LaRita Archibald
15. *A Widow's Guide to Healing: Gentle Support and Advice for the First Five Years* - Kristin Meekhof
16. *The Death of a Husband: Reflections for a Grieving Wife* - Helen Reichert Lambin
17. *'Til Suicide We Do Part: A wife's Walk of Faith Through the Unthinkable* - Jennifer Thielen
18. *When Your Soul Aches: Hope and Help for Women Who Have Lost Husbands* - Lois Mowday Rabey
19. *No Time To Say Goodbye: Surviving the Suicide Of A Loved One* - Carla Fine
20. *Healing a Spouse's Grieving Heart* - Alan D. Wolfelt
21. *Dying To Be Free: A Healing Guide for Families After a Suicide* - Beverly Cobain & Jean Larch
22. *A Widow's Journey: Reflections On Walking Alone* - Gayle Roper
23. *Finding Your Way After Your Spouse Dies* - Marta Felber
24. *Hope for an Aching Heart: Uplifting Devotions for Widows* - Margaret Nyman
25. *Grief Undone: A Journey with God and Cancer* - Elizabeth W. D. Groves
26. *The Undistracted Widow: Living For God After Losing Your Husband* - Carol W. Cornish
27. *On Becoming A Widow (When You're a Widow)* - Clarissa Start

28. *When Double Becomes Single (Charmaine's Gordon Survive and Thrive)* - Charmaine Gordon

29. *Grace for the Widow: A Journey Through the Fog Of Loss* - Joyce Rogers

30. *Suffering is My Friend & Not My Enemy* - Sharon Earnest

31. *From One Widow To Another: Conversations About The New You* - Miriam Neff

32. *Postcards from the Widows' Path - Gleaning Hope and Purpose from the Book of Ruth* - Ferree Hardy

33. *Healing a Spouse's Grieving Heart - 100 Practical Ideas After Your Husband or Wife Dies* - Alan D. Wolfelt

34. *Healing After Loss: Daily Meditations For Working Through Grief* - Martha Whitmore Hickman

35. *Heartbroken: Healing From The Loss of a Spouse* - Gary Roe

36. *Widow to Widow: Thoughtful, Practical Ideas for Rebuilding Your Life* - Genevieve Davis Ginsburg

37. *The Death of a Wife: Reflections for a Grieving Husband* - Robert Vogt

38. *When Your Soulmate Dies: A Guide To Healing Through Heroic Mourning* - Alan D. Wolfelt

39. *Grieving with Hope: Finding Comfort As You Journey Through Loss* - Samuel J IV Hodges & Kathy Leonard

40. *Second First, Live, Laugh and Love Again* - Christina Rasmussen

41. *You Took My life too...but I'm Claiming it back day by day* - Joanie Glass

42. *Melissa: A Father's Lessons from a Daughter's Suicide* - Frank Page with Lawrence Kimbrough

43. *Grieving: How to Go on Living When Someone You Love Dies* - Theresa A. Rando

44. *Confessions of a Mediocre Widow: Or How I Lost My Husband and My Sanity* - Catherine Tidd

45. *Permission to Mourn: A New Way To Do Grief* - Tom Zuba

46. *Understanding Your Suicide Grief: Ten Essential Touchstones for Finding Hope and Healing Your Heart* - Alan D. Wolfelt

47. *Happily Even After: a guide to getting through (and beyond) the grief of widowhood* - Carole Brody Fleet and Lisa Kline

48. *How to go on Living When Someone Dies* - Theresa A. Rando

49. *I'm Grieving as Fast as I can: How Young Widows and Widowers Can Cope and Heal* - Linda Feinberg

50. *Widows Wear Stilettos: A Practical and Emotional Guide for the Young Widow* - Carole Brody Fleet with Syd Harriet

51. *Bearing the Unbearable: Love, Loss, and the Heartbreaking Path of Grief* - Joanne Cacciatore and Jeffrey Rubin

52. *The Widow's Journal: Questions to Guide You through Grief and Life Planning after the loss of a Partner* - Carrie P. Freeman

53. *The Wilderness of Suicide Grief: Finding Your Way (Understanding Your Grief)* - Alan D. Wolfelt

54. *Poor Widow Me: Moments of feeling & dealing & finding the funny along the way* - Carol Scibelli

55. *Prayers for a Widow's Heart: Honest Conversations With God* - Margaret Nyman

56. *Where Do I Go From Here? Bold Living After Unwanted Change* - Miriam Neff

57. *Grieve One Day at a TIme: 365 Meditations to Help You Heal After* - Alan Wolfelt
58. *The Tender Scar: Life After the Death of a Spouse* - Richard L. Mabry
59. *The Widow* - Carla Neggers
60. *Getting to the Other Side of Grief: Overcoming the Loss of a Spouse* - Robert C. DeVries & Susan J. Zonnebelt-Smeenge
61. *Healing After Loss: Daily Meditations For Working Through Grief* - Martha Whitmore Hickman
62. *Learning to Breathe Again: Choosing Life and Finding Hope After a Shattering Loss* - Tammy Trent
63. *Beyond the Sorrow: There is Hope in the Promises of God* - Tammy Trent
64. *To Begin Again: The Journey Toward Comfort, Strength, and Faith in Difficult Times* - Naomi Levy
65. *Faith and Me: Reconstructing Your Faith After Suicide* - Charles R. Walker, Jr.
66. *And Life Comes Back: A Wife's Story of Love, Loss, and Hope Reclaimed* - Tricia Lott Williford
67. *Let's Pretend We're Normal: Adventures in Rediscovering How to be a Family* - Tricia Lott Wiliford
68. *You Can Do This: Seizing the Confidence God Offers* - Tricia Lott Williford
69. *It Will Be OK: Trusting God Through Fear and Change* - Lysa TerKeurst (for children)
70. *A Grace Disguised: How the Soul Grows Through Loss* - Jerry L. Sittser
71. *A Grief Observed* - C.S. Lewis and Madeline L'Engle

72. *The Scars That Have Shaped Me: How God Meets Us in Suffering* - Vaneetha Rendall Risner

73. *Getting To the Other Side of Grief: Overcoming the Loss of a Spouse* - Susan Zonnebelt-Smeenge

74. *Brave In A New World: A Guide to Grieving the Loss of a Spouse* - Yvonne Broady

75. *Reflections Of A Grieving Spouse: The Unexpected Journey From Loss to Hope* - H. Norman Wright

76. *Grief Diaries: Surviving Loss By Suicide* - Lynda Cheldelin Fell and Sharon Ehlers

77. *Emerging From the Heartache of Loss: How to Survive Grief and Start Living Again* - Carol Wiseman

78. *Living Again: A Personal Journey of Surviving the Loss of a Spouse* - William Wallace

79. *Grief Unveiled: A Widow's Guide to Navigating Your Journey in Life After Loss* - Sarah M. Nannen

80. *Coping When Your Spouse Dies* - Medard Laz

81. *Someone Used To Love Me: A Positive Walk Through the Loss Of a Spouse* - Susan J. Gross

82. *Grieving God's Way: The Path to Lasting Hope and Healing* - Margaret Brownly and Diantha Ain

83. *The Sun Still Rises: Surviving and Thriving after Grief and Loss* - Shawn Doyle

84. *Please Be Patient: I Am Grieving* - Gary Roe

85. *After The Loss Of A Spouse: What's Next?* - Joanne Moore and Irene Moore

86. *A New Routine: Surviving The Death Of My Spouse A to Z* - Augustus Alexander Beck

87. *All Alone: Surviving The Loss Of Your Spouse* - Kathleen Rawlings Bustin

88. *Details After Death: Navigating Logistics After A Loved One Dies* - Mark Colgan
89. *Losing A Spouse: On Love, Grief And Recovery* - Gudfinna Eydal and Anna Ingolfs
90. *Tear Soup: A Recipe For Healing After Loss* - Pat Schwiebert
91. *Faces of Grief: Overcoming the Pain of Loss* - Veronica Semenova
92. *Spouse Loss: Inspirational Stories* - Dr. Gloria Horsley and Dr. Heidi Horsley
93. *Lost My Partner: What'll I Do?* - Ruth Spector Webster and Laurie Spector
94. *Tomorrow Died Yesterday: A Survivor's Guide To The Loss Of A Spouse* - Kathleen J. Callahan, John A. Cosco
95. *From A Widow's Heart: A New Beginning* - Dorothy Brown Smith
96. *Grief Is A Journey: Finding Your Path Through Loss* - Dr. Kenneth J. Doka
97. *Beyond the Valley: Finding Hope in Life's Losses* - David Branon
98. *Finding Hope Again (Journeying Beyond Sorrow)* - Peter Millar
99. *Comfort My Soul in Christ: Death, Finding Hope Beyond The Sorrow* - Randy L. Bott
100. *MY HEART IS BROKEN: A JOURNEY OF LOSS, GRIEF AND HOPE* - Joyce Knock

M.E. Louis

BIBLE VERSES TO GUIDE YOU

The following is a list of Bible Verses that I found especially helpful during the difficult journey after my husband died. They gave me strength on my most difficult days.

If you are struggling or grieving, cut out the verses that bring you peace and hope. Put them around your house or frame them. Read them often. If you know others who are suffering, share them.

God's Words have incredible healing power. Turn to Him in your time of need.

God bless!
M.E.

"The LORD
is near to the
brokenhearted
and saves the
crushed in spirit."

Psalm 34:18 ESV

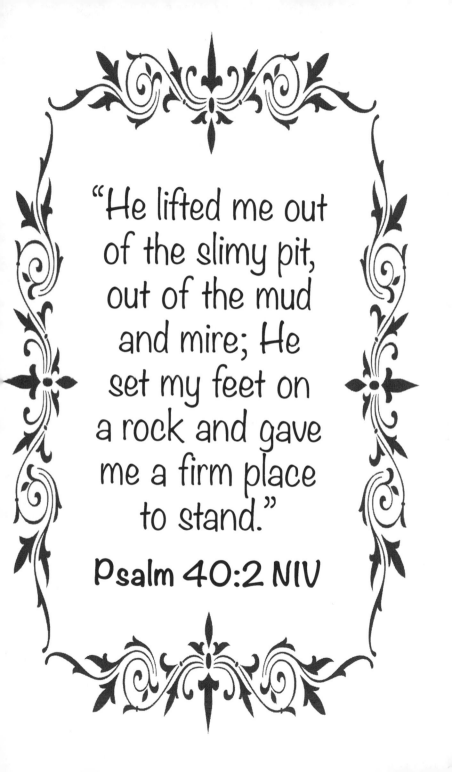

"He lifted me out of the slimy pit, out of the mud and mire; He set my feet on a rock and gave me a firm place to stand."

Psalm 40:2 NIV

"In the morning, LORD, you hear my voice; in the morning I lay my requests before you and wait expectantly."

Psalm 5:3 NIV

"Blessed be the God, and Father of our Lord Jesus Christ, the Father of mercies and God of all comfort; who comforts us in all our affliction so we may be able to comfort those who are in any affliction with the comfort with which we ourselves are comforted by God."

2 Corinthians 1:3, 4 NASB)

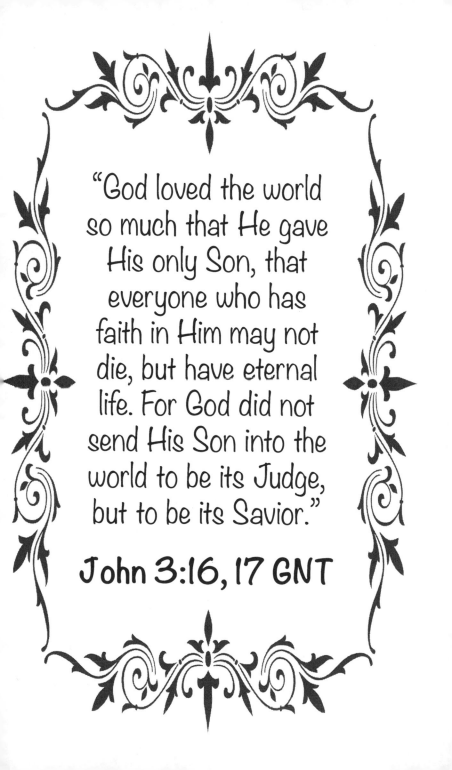

"God loved the world so much that He gave His only Son, that everyone who has faith in Him may not die, but have eternal life. For God did not send His Son into the world to be its Judge, but to be its Savior."

John 3:16, 17 GNT

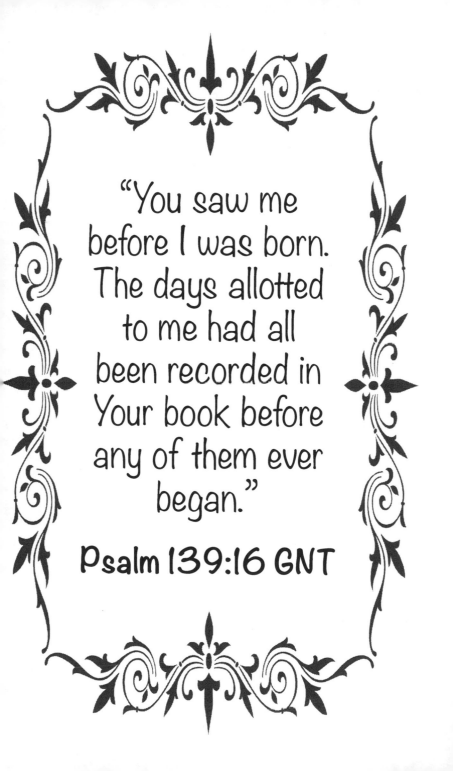

"You saw me before I was born. The days allotted to me had all been recorded in Your book before any of them ever began."

Psalm 139:16 GNT

"I love you,
LORD, my
strength."

Psalms 18:1 NIV

"I can do all
things through
Him who
strengthens me."

Philippians 4:13 NASB

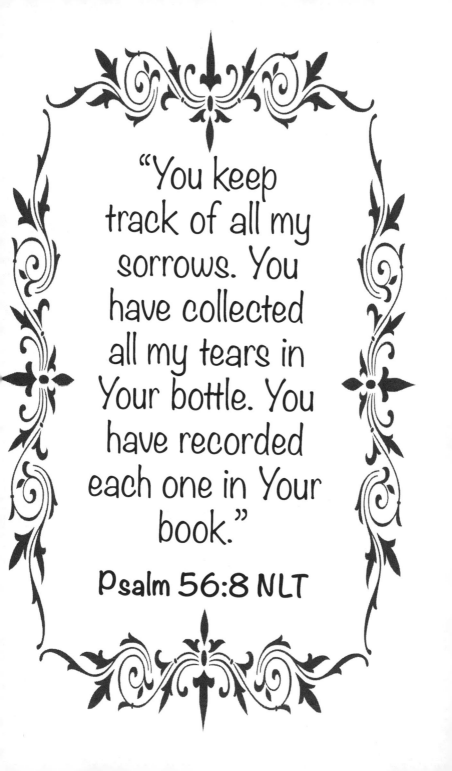

"You keep track of all my sorrows. You have collected all my tears in Your bottle. You have recorded each one in Your book."

Psalm 56:8 NLT

"God showed how much He loved us by sending His one and only Son into the world so that we might have eternal life through Him. This is real love--not that we loved God, but that He loved us and sent His Son as a sacrifice to take away our sins."

1 John 4:9-10 NLT

"Bad news won't bother them; they have decided to trust the LORD."

Psalm 112:7 CEV

"'For I know what I have planned for you', says the LORD. 'I have plans to prosper you, not to harm you. I have plans to give you a future filled with hope.'"

Jeremiah 29:11 NET

"He will wipe away every tear from their eyes, and death shall be no more, neither shall there be mourning, nor crying, nor pain anymore, for the former things have passed away."

Revelation 21:4 ESV

"Things which eye has not seen and ear has not heard, and which have not entered the heart of man, all that God has prepared for those who love Him."

I Corinthians 2:9 NASB

"The LORD directs the steps of the godly. He delights in every detail of their lives. Though they stumble, they will never fall, for the LORD holds them by the hand."

Psalm 37:23-24 NLT

"I will never desert you, nor will I ever forsake you."

Hebrews 13:5 NAS

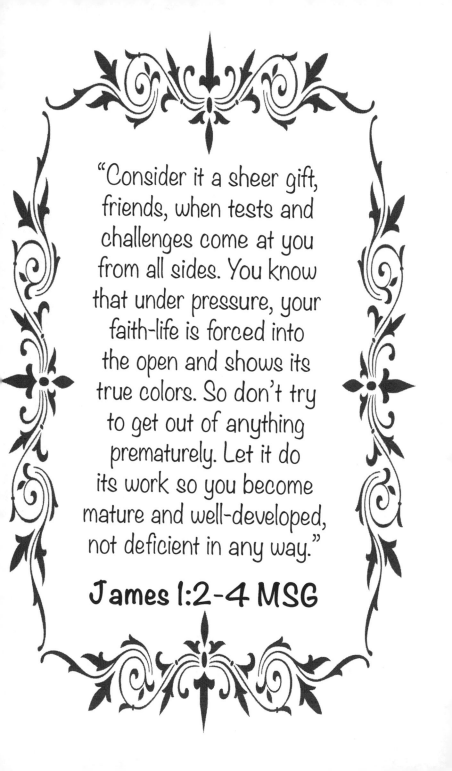

"Consider it a sheer gift, friends, when tests and challenges come at you from all sides. You know that under pressure, your faith-life is forced into the open and shows its true colors. So don't try to get out of anything prematurely. Let it do its work so you become mature and well-developed, not deficient in any way."

James 1:2-4 MSG

"Ah, LORD GOD! It is You who have made the heavens and the earth by Your great power and by Your outstretched arm! Nothing is too hard for You."

Jeremiah 32:17 ESV

"He restores my strength. He leads me down the right paths for the sake of His reputation."

Psalm 23:3 NET

"Let the morning bring me word of Your unfailing love, for I have put my trust in You. Show me the way I should go, for to You I entrust my life."

Psalm 143: 8 NIV

"For you have been my hope, Sovereign LORD, my confidence since my youth. From birth I have relied on you; you brought me forth from my mother's womb. I will ever praise you. I have become a sign to many; you are my strong refuge. My mouth is filled with your praise, declaring your splendor all day long."

Psalm 71: 5-8 NIV

"To all who mourn...
He will give beauty
for ashes; joy
instead of mourning;
praise instead of
heaviness. For God
has planted them like
strong and graceful
oaks for His own
glory."

Isaiah 61:3 TLB

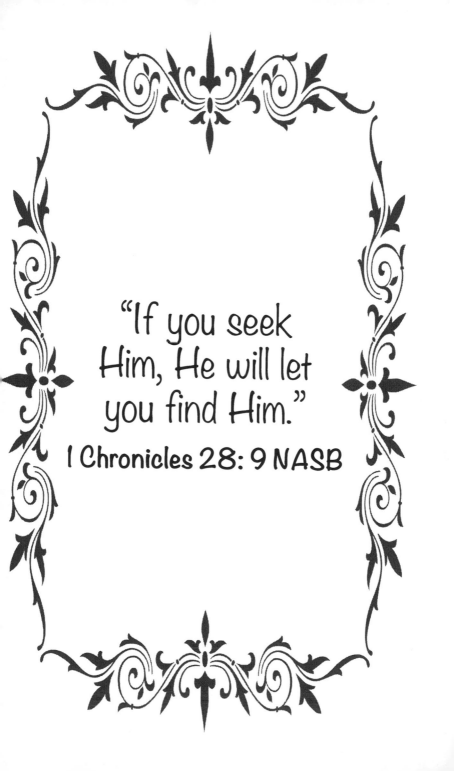

"If you seek Him, He will let you find Him."

I Chronicles 28: 9 NASB